❧ This book is about ❧

....

A MOTHER'S MEMORIES BOOK
Our Story, Our Life

A Record of Your Life, For Your Family

FLAME TREE
PUBLISHING

Completing this book 🌹

Family histories are an endlessly fascinating subject. The lives of those who have gone before us shape who we are, but we don't always find out all we can. When it comes to our parents, we don't always think to ask questions about their lives before they had children. If you can imagine the interest the early lives of your own parents would hold for you, you will realise how important it is to keep a record of your life to hand down to future generations; a record of not just the bare facts, but also your memories and emotions, your achievements and personality. Things that were everyday occurances for you will be fascinating to your children, and your story will enthral not only them, but one day their children and countless more generations to come.

This book of personal records provides a framework for your memories and history, asking questions that you might not have thought of, and providing plenty of space for photographs, momentoes and keepsakes. However you use it, this book will become a treasure trove of family folklore and a rare insight into a personal history. Enjoy the trip down memory lane and take the time to recall small details and reminisce, the result will be a rich tapestry of intriguing family history to give to your children. Whatever the story of your life, you will be able to record it here and help to give your relatives a true flavour of who you are and the times you have lived through, something no school text book can convey quite as well.

Contents

THE CHILDHOOD YEARS

FAMILY HISTORY

ADULT YEARS

IN YOUR LIFETIME

FOR MY CHILDREN

THE
CHILDHOOD
YEARS

The Beginning
Brothers & Sisters
Home Life
Social Life
Schooldays

The Beginning 🌹

What is your full name?

....

Were these names chosen for a reason?

....

....

When and where were you born?

....

How much did you weigh at birth?

....

PLACE YOUR PHOTO HERE

PLACE YOUR PHOTO HERE

How old were your parents when you were born?

Brothers & Sisters

How many brothers and sisters did you have? ....

NAME	DATE BORN	PLACE BORN
....	....	....
....	....	....
....	....	....
....	....	....

Who was the best behaved?

....

Who was the naughtiest?

....

Who did you fight with?

....

Who did you get on well with?

....

PLACE YOUR PHOTO HERE

What do you particularly remember about your brothers and sisters from your childhood?

....

....

....

....

PLACE YOUR PHOTO HERE

What were their occupations as adults?

....

....

....

What are your memories of them in adult life?

....

....

....

Home Life 🌹

Where did you live when you were young?

....

Did you have a bedroom of your own? ....

What do you remember about your home?

....

....

....

....

Did you have a garden? ....

Did you move when you were young? ....

Where else did you live?

PLACE   DATE

....

....

....

....

What are your earliest memories?

....

....

....

....

What was your favourite toy?

....

....

What games did you play?

....

....

PLACE YOUR PHOTO HERE

Home Life

Did you have any pets?

....

PLACE YOUR PHOTO HERE

What were your favourite and least favourite meals?

FAVOURITE

....

....

....

LEAST FAVOURITE

....

....

....

Did you ever argue with your parents?

....

....

Were you given pocket money? ....

If so, how much was it?   Did you have to earn it?

....

....

....

What did you like to spend it on?

....

....

Did you do any chores around the house in order to earn your pocket money?

....

....

Which was your best birthday and why was it so special?

....

....

What was the best present you ever received? ....

Did you have any family traditions at Christmas?

....

....

Social Life

Were you allowed to listen to music? ....

What sort of music did you like?

....

....

PLACE YOUR PHOTO HERE

Were you allowed to wear what you wanted?

....

Can you remember the first clothes you bought with your own money?

....

....

Did you have a favourite actor or actress?

....

....

Was there anywhere you used to go to regularly in the evenings or at weekends?

....

....

Who was your first kiss with?

How old were you?

....

....

Who was your first boyfriend?

How long were you together?

....

....

Schooldays

Describe your first school. How old were you when you went there?

What do you remember about your teachers? Did you like it there?

....

....

....

Which school did you move on to after that?

....

How did you get to school? ....

Did you have a best friend? ....

Who were your other friends?

NAMES

....

....

....

....

....

....

What were your favourite and least favourite subjects?

FAVOURITE   LEAST FAVOURITE

....

....

Who was your favourite teacher and why?

....

....

How much homework were you given?   ....

Did you have to wear a uniform? Describe it.

....

....

PLACE YOUR PHOTO HERE

Schooldays

Were you well-behaved or did you ever get into trouble at school?

....

Did you learn any musical instruments? ....

Were you good at sports?   What did you play?

....

Did you have a part-time or Saturday job when you were older?

....

How old were you when you left school? ....

PLACE YOUR PHOTO HERE

Did you go on to further studies? ....

If so, where did you go and what did you study?

....

If not, what did you do?

....

What qualifications did you gain?

SUBJECT

....

....

....

QUALIFICATION

....

....

....

What are your best memories of this time?

....

....

....

....

....

....

....

FAMILY HISTORY

Your Parents
Your Grandparents

Your Parents 🌹

What was your father's name? ....

When and where was he born?

DATE BORN   PLACE BORN

....

PLACE YOUR PHOTO HERE

What was his occupation? ....

Describe his appearance. What were his interests and hobbies?

....

....

What was your mother's full name before she was married? ....

When and where was she born?

DATE BORN   PLACE BORN

....

Describe her appearance. What were her interests and hobbies?

....

....

Did she have a job? Did she continue to work after her marriage?

....

What are your fondest memories of her?

....

....

PLACE YOUR PHOTO HERE

Your Grandparents

What were your father's parents' names?

NAME   DATE BORN   PLACE BORN

....

....

What were their occupations?

GRANDFATHER   GRANDMOTHER

....

When did they die? How old were they?

GRANDFATHER   GRANDMOTHER

....

PLACE YOUR PHOTO HERE

PLACE YOUR PHOTO HERE

24

What were your mother's parents' names?

NAME   DATE BORN   PLACE BORN

....

....

What were their occupations?

GRANDFATHER   GRANDMOTHER

....

When did they die? How old were they?

GRANDFATHER   GRANDMOTHER

....

PLACE YOUR PHOTO HERE

ADULT YEARS

Working Life
When You Met
Your Wedding
Married Life

Working Life

What was your first full-time job? ....

Did you enjoy it?

....

....

How much were you paid? ....

Was it easy or hard to make ends meet?

....

....

How did you travel to work?   What hours did you work?

....

What were your colleagues like?

....

....

How long did you stay in your first job?

....

Where have you worked since?

....

....

Where have you most enjoyed working?

....

....

What did you want to be when you were a child and why?

....

....

....

When You Met 🌹

How did you first meet your future husband or partner?

....

....

....

How old were you both? ....

What were your first impressions of each other?

....

....

Where did you go on your first date?

....

....

....

....

....

....

....

How long were you together before you got engaged? ....

How long was your engagement? ....

How did the proposal take place?

....

....

....

....

Describe the engagement ring.

....

....

PLACE YOUR PHOTO HERE

PLACE YOUR PHOTO HERE

Your Wedding 🌹

What was the date of your wedding? ....

How old were you both when you got married?

....

Where did the ceremony take place? ....

PLACE YOUR PHOTO HERE

What did you wear on your wedding day?

....

....

Who was the best man?   Did you have any bridesmaids?

....

How many guests came? ....

Did you have a reception? ....

Where was it held?   What did you eat?

....

....

....

....

Did you dance to a special song?

....

What are your main memories of your wedding day?

....

....

Did you have a honeymoon?

....

....

....

....

....

....

PLACE YOUR PHOTO HERE

Married Life 🌹

Where was your first home together? Describe it.

....

....

....

Why did you choose to live there?

....

....

How long did you live there? ....

How long did you wait before having children? ....

PLACE YOUR PHOTO HERE

How many children did you have? ....

NAME	DATE BORN	BIRTH WEIGHT
....	....	....
....	....	....
....	....	....
....	....	....

What are your favourite memories from when they were small?

....

....

Was there anywhere you went to often on family holidays?

....

....

PLACE YOUR PHOTO HERE

IN YOUR LIFETIME

▽

Friends & Homes
Holidays
In Your Lifetime

Friends & Homes 🌹

Who have been your best friends during your life?

....

How did you meet them and get to know them?

....

Why do you think you get on so well?

....

....

What are the happiest memories you have of your friends?

....

PLACE YOUR PHOTO HERE

PLACE YOUR PHOTO HERE

Can you remember all the places you have lived during your lifetime?

ADDRESS	DATE	WHO LIVED THERE WITH YOU
....	....	....
....	....	....
....	....	....
....	....	....
....	....	....
....	....	....
....	....	....

Which was your favourite place to live and why?

....

....

....

PLACE YOUR PHOTO HERE

Holidays

What sort of holidays did you go on as a child?

....

Where was your favourite place to visit as a child and why?

....

....

PLACE YOUR PHOTO HERE

Have you been back to any of these places with your own children? Was it as good as you remembered?

....

....

Did you go on any memorable holidays after you left school?

....

....

Have you ever lived in another country? Did you enjoy it?

....

....

PLACE YOUR PHOTO HERE

What has been your favourite place to visit as an adult and why?

....

....

Where would you like to visit that you haven't yet been to?

....

In Your Lifetime ✿

Have you ever met any famous people? What were the circumstances?

....

....

....

Have you witnessed any exciting or significant historical events?

....

....

What have been the most important historical events to take place in your lifetime?

....

....

PLACE YOUR PHOTO HERE

Do you have any regrets?

....

....

What are you most proud of?

....

....

What is the best piece of advice you ever received?

....

....

....

Which person in your life has had the best influence on you?

....

....

....

If you could choose any occupation for a single day, what would it be and why?

....

....

....

FOR MY
CHILDREN

For My Children

For My Children 🌹

What was the child you are writing this for like as a baby?

....

....

What is your fondest memory of them as a baby?

....

....

What did they enjoy doing most as a youngster?

....

....

PLACE YOUR PHOTO HERE

PLACE YOUR PHOTO HERE

If you could give them one piece of advice, what would it be?

....

....

....

Publisher and Creative Director: Nick Wells
Project Editor: Chelsea Edwards
Designer: Lucy Robins and Jake
Picture Research: Frances Bodiam

FLAME TREE PUBLISHING
Crabtree Hall, Crabtree Lane
Fulham, London SW6 6TY
United Kingdom

www.flametreepublishing.com

First published in 2009

11 13 12 10

5 7 9 10 8 6 4

Picture Credits

All images are courtesy of the Fine Art Photographic Library
Front cover and page 1: *A Summer's Day on Hornbaek Beach, Denmark,* by Frants Peder Diderik Henningsen (1850–1908)
Page 2 (t to b): *In the Schoolroom,* by Theophile Emmanuel Duverger (b. 1821); *Happy Days,* by Frederick Morgan (1856–1927)
Pages 4–5: *A Lively Haul,* by Frederick Morgan (1856–1927)
Page 7: *Jeune Femme et Bebe,* by Henry Jules Jean Geoffroy (1853–1924)
Page 8: *Shrimping,* by William Marshall Brown (1863–1936)
Page 9: *Playing on the Beach,* by Thomas Liddall Armitage (d. 1924)
Page 11: *Playing on the Beach,* by Edith Hume (d. 1906)
Back cover and page 12: *A Fairy World,* by Frederick Morgan (1856–1927)
Page 14: *The Letter,* by Eugene De Blaas (1843–1931)
Page 15: *After the swim at Hornbaek Beach, Denmark,* by Paul Fischer (1860–1934)
Page 16: *In the Schoolroom,* by Theophile Emmanuel Duverger (b. 1821)
Page 17: *Going to School,* by James Hayllar (1829–1920)
Page 18: *In the Schoolroom,* by Basile De Loose (1809–85)
Page 19: *The Student,* by Elias Molineaux Bancroft (d. 1924)
Pages 20–21: *Her First Steps,* by Hermann Sondermann (1832–1901)
Page 22: *The Family Reunion,* by Gustav Pope (1852–1910)
Page 23: *Happy Days,* by Frederick Morgan (1856–1927)
Page 25: *The Fledglings,* by James Hardy (1832–89)
Pages 26–27: *La Jolie Artiste, Le Pont Des Arts, Paris, France,* by Jean Beraud (1849–1936)
Page 29: *A Helpful Sister,* by Edith Hume (d. 1906)
Page 30: *A Love Match,* by Jan Van Beers (1852–1927)
Page 32: *Betrothed,* by William Savage Cooper (d. 1926)
Page 33: *The Wedding,* by John Morgan (1823–86)
Page 34: *The Introduction,* by Emily Crawford (fl. 1869–1900)
Page 35: *Picking Apples,* by Frederick Morgan (1856–1927)
Pages 36–37: *Playing with Mother,* by William Kay Blacklock (1872–1924)
Page 39: *A Berkshire Cottage,* by Helen Allingham (1848–1926)
Page 40: *Testing the Water,* by Percy Tarrant (d. 1934)
Page 41: *Testing the Water,* by Percy Tarrant (d. 1934)
Page 42: *A Stitch in Time,* by William Kay Blacklock (1872–1924)
Pages 44–45: *La Maternite,* by Louis-Emile Adan (1839–1937)
Page 47: *Picking Apples,* by Frederick Morgan (1856–1927)

A CIP record for this book is available from the British Library.

ISBN 978 1 84786 547 2

Printed in China

❦ This book was completed on ❦

....